$\mathcal{D}_i$

N(

Compiled by Julia Skinner

With particular reference to the work of Frank Meeres

THE FRANCIS FRITH COLLECTION

www.francisfrith.com

First published in the United Kingdom in 2012 by The Francis Frith Collection®

This edition published exclusively for Identity Books in 2012 ISBN 978-1-84589-684-3

British Library Cataloguing in Publication Data

Did You Know? Norwich - A Miscellany
Compiled by Julia Skinner
With particular reference to the work of Frank Meeres

The Francis Frith Collection
Oakley Business Park,
Wylye Road, Dinton,
Wiltshire SP3 5EU
Tel: +44 (0) 1722 716 376
Email: info@francisfrith.co.uk
www.francisfrith.com

Printed and bound in Malaysia
Contains material sourced from responsibly managed forests

Front Cover: **NORWICH, DAVEY PLACE 1922** 72602p
Frontispiece: **NORWICH, THE CASTLE 1890** 24043
Contents: **NORWICH, THE POST OFFICE AND PRINCE OF WALES ROAD 1896** 37362

The colour-tinting is for illustrative purposes only, and is not intended to be historically accurate

CONTENTS

INTRODUCTION

Some years ago, the slogan 'Welcome to Norwich – a fine city' was chosen to adorn the city entry road signs. It is an attractive and historic place, despite the damage caused by Second World War bombing and modern development. Like all modern cities, it is now surrounded by suburbs in which can be found the remains of older villages.

The first real settlements in what is now Norwich were Anglo-Saxon. These grew to become a fortified burgh which by about AD920 had its own mint and was known as 'Norwic', meaning 'the north settlement' or 'the north trading port'. The Saxon town centred on Tombland, the enormous market place to which all the oldest roads in the city still lead, which was then twice the size it is today. Around it was a planned town of parallel blocks, with a small church at each crossroads. Several of these churches had round towers rather than square – there are still some churches with round towers in Norwich, for example St Mary Coslany and St Benedict, which may reflect the influence of the area's historical trading links across the North Sea with Denmark and north Germany. Norwich continued to grow, and by the time of the Norman Conquest in 1066 it could sustain about 40 churches, and was the third largest port on the east coast of England after London and York.

After the Norman Conquest, the new rulers imposed upon the Saxon town the three elements that most people now associate with Norwich – the castle, the market place and the cathedral. The Norman castle was built at the highest spot in the town, and its building involved destroying a large number of Saxon houses. The castle keep – a cube almost 30 metres (95 feet) deep and 23 metres (70 feet) high – is the largest in England apart from the Tower of London. The bailey, or outer defence, stretched over the area now known as Castle Mall, down to the 'Steam Packet', and included the site of the Royal Hotel, and also the area covered by shops on both sides of the street now called Castle Meadow. The provision market was moved out of Tombland to a new site, that it still occupies today. There were many other markets within the city, some of whose names live on as street names, such as wood at Timberhill, hay on the Haymarket, pigs at Hog Hill and horses at Horsefair, off St Faith's Lane. The cathedral was also imposed upon the old Saxon town, and half of Tombland was taken over by the monks and included within their new precinct wall. The cathedral has had many adventures over the centuries, including being set on fire by angry citizens in 1272 after a dispute over the fair in Tombland. The present spire was added after an earlier one collapsed during a thunderstorm in 1461. Rising to 96 metres (315 feet), it is the second tallest in England, beaten only by the spire of Salisbury Cathedral.

The city spread rapidly and, from the mid 13th until the mid 14th centuries, stone city walls were built with no less than 11 fortified gateways. The walls, stretches of which survive today, were about 2.5 miles long. They protected only three sides of the large medieval city, as the fourth side was protected by a mile of the bank of the River Wensum. This river was once a vital waterway for the carrying of fleeces and woollen produce, for Norwich was one of the great weaving centres of medieval England and became one of the country's wealthiest cities based on the wool trade. Indeed, until 1700 Norwich was the second largest and wealthiest city after London.

One of Norwich's great benefactors in the later 19th century was John Gurney, a local banker, whose two key contributions to the city are still visible today. In 1880, when the cathedral gave the city 185 acres of Mousehold for use as a 'People's Park', Gurney gave £1,000 to make it accessible and for the laying out of cricket pitches. During his year as mayor he provided work for hundreds of unemployed men, laying out a new road across the Heath, now called Gurney Road in his honour. His other achievement was turning Norwich Castle into a museum – John Gurney was a leading light in establishing the museum, offering £5,000 of his own money towards the scheme.

The greatest feature of Norwich is the sense of history that pervades the city. In whichever area you find yourself, people have been living and working there for thousands of years. The Park and Ride car park at Harford, for example, is on a site formerly used for

Neolithic flint working, with Bronze Age pits and ditches, a Roman barn and a Saxon farmstead. Prehistoric activity was also discovered during archaeological work at Norwich football ground before the building of the new Jarrold Stand. In the Mesolithic period (10,000–4,000 BC) this site was a sandbank or island in the river on which flint was worked by the earliest known inhabitants of the area we now call Norwich. To walk through Norwich nowadays is to visit a town where the old and the new stand side by side. Visitors to the cathedral now find a shop and restaurant, blending in with the ancient architecture of the close. The former cattle market area has been converted into one of the boldest and most exciting shopping precincts in Britain, Castle Mall, where the shops are actually underground, in an enormous hole, covered partly by a huge roof, but mainly by a public park. The River Wensum, which runs through the heart of Norwich and was once a key factor in its growth, is being developed once more as a means of transport, both for leisure trips and for daily commuter traffic.

With its new developments and leisure areas as well as its older, historic attractions, Norwich in the 21st century has a lot to be proud of – a fine city indeed!

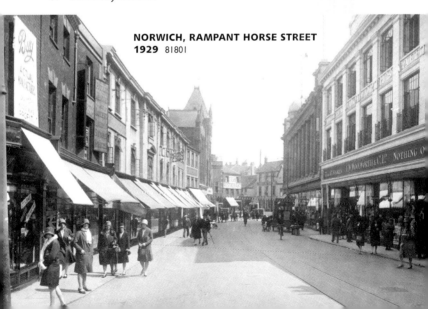

NORWICH, RAMPANT HORSE STREET 1929 81801

NORFOLK DIALECT
WORDS AND PHRASES

'Afront' – in front.

'Ahind' – behind.

'Atwin' – between.

'Bishy barney bee' – a ladybird.

'Dodman' – a snail.

'Dudder' – to shiver.

'Dwile' – a floor cloth.

'Harnser' – a heron.

'I'll get wrong!' – I'll get told off!

'Lollop' – to move along slowly.

'Luggy' – deaf.

'Lummox' – a clumsy or awkward person.

'Mardle' – to gossip or chat.

'Mavish' – a thrush.

'Mawkin' – a scarecrow.

'Mawther' – a young woman.

'On the huh' – slanted, not level or straight.

'Squit' – talking nonsense.

'Titty-totty' – very small.

'Uhmtie-tump' – a mole hill.

'Warmint' – vermin, or a varmint, a troublesome person.

HAUNTED NORWICH

Cow Tower (see photograph 28158, page 13) was built on the River Wensum near Bishop Bridge in the 14th century to defend a curve of the river where the city wall ended, and was used as the water toll gate where taxes were collected on vessels plying the river. No one now knows why it was called 'Cow Tower' but it is the oldest surviving brick building in Norwich, and is reputedly haunted by Old Blunderhazard, a ghostly rider who gallops past on Christmas Eve.

Ghost hunters looking for haunted pubs in Norwich are somewhat spoiled for choice! The Adam and Eve at Bishopgate, believed to be the oldest public house in Norwich, is said to be haunted by the ghost of Lord Sheffield who died at the inn in 1549. The Coachmakers Arms in St Stephen's Road is haunted by a phantom highwayman who has been seen standing at the bar. A ghostly woman dressed in black clothing has also been seen gliding down the staircase. Another of Norwich's oldest pubs is now called Henry's, in Haymarket; it has previously been known by a number of names, including (originally) the Holy Lamb, the Lamb Inn and the Rat and Parrot. This pub's resident ghost is believed to be the shade of John Aggas, a former landlord who was murdered there in 1797 after an argument with his brother-in-law, who he had discovered in the cellar offering free drinks to his friends. The ghost has been seen sitting in a chair by a window of the establishment. The Maid's Head Hotel at Tombland is haunted by the grey-clad ghost of a former maid who worked there. She appears to be an elderly woman, and her appearances are always followed by the scent of lavender. The ghost of a young boy, believed to have died in a fire in the pub's cellar at some time in the past, is said to roam the Wild Man pub in Bedford Street. A mysterious young boy has been seen running through the bar area and up the stairs, and the unexplained sound of beer barrels rolling across the cellar floor has been heard late at night, although no one is there…

NORWICH, LONDON STREET 1919 69052

A mysterious grey lady is said to haunt Augustine Steward House at Tombland, formerly a medieval merchant's trading house. She is believed to be the unquiet shade of a young woman who died there after the townspeople boarded up the house during a plague epidemic; unbeknown to them, she had survived the plague which had killed the other occupants of the house, but she starved to death, unable to get out of the house.

Norwich Castle is reputed to be haunted by the ghost of an elderly woman wearing a long black dress. The first reports of the spectre were in the 1820s, when prisoners at the castle were terrified by the apparition, but ghostly activity still seems to be occurring there – in recent years, staff at the castle have reported seeing a mysterious old lady in the grounds, who appears to be floating a few inches above ground level as she moves along.

NORWICH MISCELLANY

The Norfolk Record Office in the modern Archive Centre holds over 12 million documents, including a charter dating from the year 1090.

The Viking king Sweyn Forkbeard sailed up to Norwich in 1004 and burnt the city.

Norwich in the Middle Ages was a city of churches. Before the Reformation in the 16th century there were over 50 churches within the walls of medieval Norwich, of which over 30 still survive today.

The city charter of 1404 gave Norwich a mayor for the first time, and its new civic pride led to a building project that can still be seen today, the Guildhall. This was begun in 1407 and took over 40 years to complete. The master mason who built the Guildhall, John Marowe, was paid sixpence a day for his work. He may well have been responsible for the chequered pattern of limestone and black flint which can be seen on the east wall (see photograph 81799, opposite).

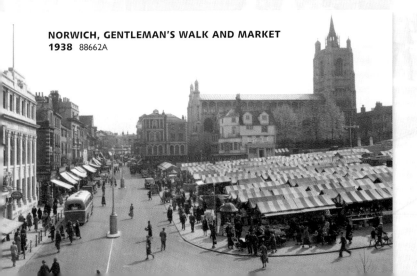

**NORWICH, GENTLEMAN'S WALK AND MARKET
1938** 88662A

NORWICH, THE GUILDHALL AND THE WAR MEMORIAL 1929 81799

Photograph 88664 (below) shows one of the pair of boom towers beside the River Wensum. The boom towers were part of the medieval defences of the city. At night, a chain was strung between them across the river, thus preventing a surprise attack by water. Unfortunately, the tower seen in this photograph is now only half the height it was when this photograph was taken in 1938.

A drain cover in Tombland Alley is the only one in the city to bear the name of the firm of Thomas Crapper, the Victorian engineers of such works, and a reminder of the great 19th-century achievement in bringing water into and taking sewage out of the houses of Norwich.

People hanged outside Norwich Castle in the 18th century were buried in the churchyard of St Michael's at Thorn.

NORWICH, BOOM TOWERS AND CARROW BRIDGE 1938 88664

NORWICH, OLD COW TOWER AND THE RIVER WENSUM 1891 28158

A significant event for Norwich occurred in 1549 when 'Kett's Rebellion' broke out. In fact, it was not a rebellion at all but an outburst of non-violent protest by the poor and the lower middle class, led by Robert Kett of Wymondham. Several thousand people camped out on Mousehold Heath, at the top of what is now Gas Hill. They were eventually crushed by Swiss mercenaries under the Earl of Warwick. The battle took place at a site called Dussindale, but it is not known for certain where this was. The Council have named a new housing estate three miles east of Norwich 'Dussindale', but evidence suggests that the battle was actually fought on Mousehold Heath, probably in the Long Valley to the north of Gurney Road. Following defeat, Kett was captured and hanged from the keep of Norwich Castle. The city ordered that a local holiday be established celebrating Kett's downfall, and all the shops in the city were to close on 27 August 'from henceforward forever'! Attitudes to the rebellion have changed over the centuries, and on the 400th anniversary of Kett's death, a plaque was put up at the Castle in his honour. During Kett's Rebellion, damage was caused by Kett's gunner to the top of Cow Tower, which is still visible today (see photograph 28158, above).

A key development in the city occurred in June 1566, when 30 master craftsmen from Europe were invited to come to Norwich to give a kick-start to the weaving trade. This was certainly needed: exports of cloth had sunk from 2,000 or more units a year in the 1530s to a mere 36 units in 1561. Of the craftsmen, 24 were Dutch and six were Walloons (a French-speaking people from the area now known as Belgium). Within five years over 4,000 of their countrymen had joined them in the city. These immigrants brought many things to Norwich, including banknotes, tulips and their favourite pet, the canary, a bird which has now become so closely associated with the city that Norwich City Football Club play in canary yellow colours, nicknamed 'The Canaries'. Over the years, local breeders have established a specific type of these delightful little birds, known as the Norwich Canary.

The word 'Strangers' is used in Norwich to refer to the Dutch and Walloon weavers who came to the city in the reign of Queen Elizabeth I (see above). The Dutch and the French-speaking Walloons had their own churches at first, but within two or three generations had merged into Norwich's cultural mix. It is not known when or why the historic building at Charing Cross in Norwich became known as Strangers' Hall (see photograph 69049, opposite). However, its owner in the mid 15th century, the wealthy grocer Nicholas Sotherton (who was mayor of the city in 1539), was one of the men who invited the Strangers to Norwich. He also allowed some of them to settle in property adjoining this building. Strangers' Hall is now used as a museum.

The first public library in Britain was set up in the porch of St Andrew's Hall in Norwich in 1608.

When Joseph Oxley, a glass bottle salesman, visited Norwich in 1781 he was most impressed by the fact that the city had 12 gaols. He also commented that 'the chief trade here is stockings, bays [baize, a sort of cloth], serges, shallooons and other worsted stuff', a comment on Norwich's textile industry.

By the 18th century, shoemaking was growing in importance as another local industry in Norwich. Some new ideas in the shoe trade were first put into practice in Georgian Norwich. James Smith, who had a leather shop on the Market for 40 years, seems to have had a 'cunning scheme' in the 1790s, and one which changed the nature of shopping. He is said to have been the first person in the world to think of selling boots and shoes in stock sizes, rather than having each customer individually measured. His grandson, Charles Winter was also an innovator, as he was the first Norwich shoemaker to use the sewing machine for closing uppers. The business later passed to the Southall family, one of the most prominent shoe-makers in the city, especially famed for their 'Start-Rite' children's shoes. In 1861, some 3,000 people in the city worked in the boot and shoe trade; ten years later the figure was 6,000. Even as recently as 1971 there were still 9,000 people in Norwich employed in shoemaking.

NORWICH, STRANGERS' HALL 1919   69049

NORWICH
A MISCELLANY

NORWICH
THE CATHEDRAL AND PULLS FERRY
1891 28157

NORWICH, MAID'S HEAD HOTEL 1929 81813

Pine Banks Tower at Thorpe St Andrew was commissioned by the Norwich solicitor John Taylor. The historian Walter Rye says it was known as Taylor's Folly for its function was to enable Taylor to indulge in several of his hobbies. He was a keen astronomer and kept his telescope in the room at the top of the tower, and he also held chess tournaments there. Today the tower is still a prominent feature among the trees on Thorpe ridge. From a nearby public path an inscription recording the visit of Queen Kapiolani of Hawaii can be seen. She came to England in 1887 for the Golden Jubilee of Queen Victoria and climbed this tower on 6 June. The Queen and her daughter, Princess Liliukalani, were guests of Captain Steward of Rackheath Park, who had known them when he was in Hawaii. They went to a service in Norwich Cathedral and on the following day had a formal lunch at the Guildhall, visited the Castle (not yet a museum), and then went on to Pine Banks, where they were delighted to see the Hawaiian flag flying from the tower.

Bishop's Bridge, built before 1340, is probably the oldest bridge in England still in daily use. There was a fortified gatehouse on the bridge until the 18th century, and the semicircular projection on the left marks where one of its outer turrets stood. The central arch sports the arms of the city – a lion and a castle. In August 1912 around 16 centimetres (6 inches) of rain fell in Norwich in 12 hours. One man, Harry Abel, saved the medieval Bishop's Bridge from destruction by clearing fallen trees from the river that threatened to overwhelm it.

When Anglia Television came to Norwich, their mast at Mendlesham was the tallest man-made structure in Britain.

NORWICH, BISHOPS BRIDGE 1891 28159

NORWICH, WESTLEGATE 1890 24044

Norwich came under a brief period of Viking rule in the Dark Ages. Despite ruling Norwich for less than 50 years (between AD870 and AD917), the Vikings have left their mark on the city. The best place to see this is at the so-called 'Viking pillar', an interpretative sign erected under the auspices of city archaeologist Brian Ayers. This is at the junction of Magdalen Street and Colegate. Street names like Colegate are one of the main legacies of the Vikings in Norwich. The 'gate' part of the word is taken from the Scandinavian word 'gata' meaning 'way', and has nothing to do with gates as we now think of them. Cole is a personal name, and Colegate thus means 'Cole's Way'. Other examples of such names are Fishergate, the street where the fishermen lived, and Westlegate, the street where wassal (high-quality white bread) was sold.

Mousehold Heath once covered 2,500 hectares (6,000 acres) and extended into eight parishes. It now covers 75 hectares (185 acres).

Edward Elgar composed and performed his 'Sea Pictures' especially for the Norwich Festival of 1899.

Norwich once had a cinema with a thatched roof. It closed after the 'talkies' were introduced because it had never been fitted up for sound.

THORPE ST ANDREW, ON THE RIVER 1919 69076

The Great Hospital at Bishopgate in Norwich was founded by Walter de Suffield, Bishop of Norwich, in October 1249. He was another of the city's many lovers of sport: when he died he left his pack of hounds to the King! The Hospital was intended to provide shelter for up to 30 chaplains. In addition, 13 poor people were allowed to warm themselves at the fire in winter, and to have one meal a day throughout the year. The choir of the Hospital church is made up of 252 wooden panels, on each of which is painted an imperial eagle. It is said that these were painted in honour of Queen Anne of Bohemia, the wife of King Richard II. The King and Queen visited Norwich in 1383, when the citizens were stunned to see Queen Anne ride side-saddle, the first person ever to do so in Norwich.

Part of the medieval city wall of Norwich lies buried under Prince of Wales Road.

NORWICH, BISHOPGATE AND ST HELEN'S CHURCH 1921 70881

NORWICH, CATTLE MARKET AND CASTLE 1896 37359

Norwich Corporation paid £4,900 for Eaton Park in 1907. The ponds and pavilions were created in the 1920s as part of a scheme to provide work for the unemployed. The park was formally opened by the Prince of Wales in 1928.

A musket ball fired by one of Cromwell's troops during the Civil War of the 17th century can be seen embedded in a tomb in Norwich Cathedral.

6,700 American airmen stationed in Norfolk were killed in action during the Second World War. It was decided that they should be remembered in a living Memorial Library, and this is now an important part of the Millennium Library in Norwich.

NORWICH, ELM HILL 1929 81806

NORWICH, DAVEY PLACE 1922 72602

The phrase 'Norwich – a fine old city' was created by the writer George Borrow, born at East Dereham and educated at Norwich Grammar School. The phrase occurs several times in his book 'Lavengro'. It has been used since as the title for several books and also on road signs welcoming people into the city, although the word 'old' is always left out!

In the 19th century Norwich had a public house for every day of the year.

The Church of St John Maddermarket is named after the madder, a red dye obtained from the madder plant, which was once traded in the area.

The first printer in Norwich was a Dutch immigrant, Anthony Solen, who arrived from Brabant in 1569. Solen combined printing with the selling of wine from the Rhineland. Another immigrant from the Netherlands, Giles Nevageer, a bookbinder, possibly worked in collaboration with Solen. Norwich has a further claim to printing fame – the first newspaper in England outside London was published here, the 'Norwich Post', which was issued in 1703 by Francis Burges.

NORWICH, DIOCESAN TRAINING COLLEGE 1901 46679

In the Middle Ages, there was a strong Jewish community living in Norwich. Most members lived around the areas now known as White Lion Street and Haymarket. They worshipped at a synagogue which was located in the Haymarket area. Jews were expelled from Norwich (and everywhere else in England) by Edward I in 1290, and archaeological evidence suggests that the medieval synagogue was burnt down at this time. A memory of the Jewish presence in Norwich in medieval times is preserved in at least one building, the Music House in King Street, which was lived in by a Jewish family named Jurnet – the cellar (or undercroft) of this building is now Jurnet's Bar.

The Bethel Hospital in Norwich was the first asylum for the mentally ill outside London. It was founded by Mary Chapman in 1714.

NORWICH, OLD PALACE AT HEIGHAM 1891 28176

The Old Palace at Heigham shown in photograph 28176 (opposite) is called a palace because in the 17th century the Bishop of Norwich, Joseph Hall, lived there after being thrown out of the Bishop's Palace in the Cathedral Close by supporters of Oliver Cromwell. He died here and was buried in the nearby church of St Bartholomew. The house later became the Dolphin Inn. It was badly damaged in the Second World War but has since been restored.

NORWICH, THE CATHEDRAL, THE CHOIR WEST 1919   69043

Ten people died on Good Friday 1817 when the steam packet to Yarmouth blew up near Foundry Bridge.

In 1589 the Elizabethan seaman Francis Drake borrowed the 'Waits' – the Norwich city musicians – to provide entertainment for his men on a voyage to Spain.

When Queen Elizabeth I visited Norwich in 1578, her retinue brought the plague with them to the city from London.

The Dukes of Norfolk once had a great palace in the city, extending to the river along what is now Duke Street, under the sites of the telephone exchange and the former St Andrew's car park. The palace was pulled down in 1711 after the Duke had an argument with the mayor of Norwich and stormed out of the city. Until 1958 the entrance to the Board School in Duke Street was graced by two lions that were possibly rescued from the palace, but, sadly, these too have since disappeared. The Dukes were Roman Catholics and the chapel of the palace survived until the 1970s, but by this time it was being used as a billiards club!

The first telephone communication between Norwich and London was a cornet solo played by a member of the Carrow Works Band in 1878. The first telephone exchange in the city was opened in 1883.

NORWICH, PRINCE OF WALES ROAD 1935 86746

NORWICH, PRINCE OF WALES ROAD 1919 69058

A 200-year-old tunnel exists beneath Thorpe Road, built to allow the Harvey family access to their water-meadows. It is now a haven for bats.

The first motor car arrived in Norwich in November 1896. It belonged to the owner of a visiting menagerie, who allowed the curious to take a ride in it. Thirty years later, on 26 August 1927, the 10,000th Norwich motor car was registered.

During the Second World War, rodeos were held at Carrow Road football ground to entertain the American airmen who were stationed in the area.

NORWICH, SAMSON AND HERCULES HOUSE, TOMBLAND 1929 81810

Photograph 81810 (opposite) shows Samson and Hercules House at Tombland; this house was probably built by Christopher Jay, mayor of the city in 1657, and an MP for Norwich from 1661. The house appears to have been built during his year as mayor. The figures of Samson and Hercules graced the front of the house from that date until 1789, when they were taken down. Two figures were again placed at the front of the house in 1900, when George Cubitt restored the building, but Hercules, on the right of the photograph with the lion's skin round his waist, is in fact a late 19th-century copy of the original. Samson on the left hand side of the photograph, who holds a lamb in his left hand, is the same statue first put there almost 350 years ago.

The name of Ber Street means 'the street on the ridge'. In the early 20th century up to 3,000 cattle were driven along Ber Street on a Saturday to the Cattle Market in the Castle Ditches.

NORWICH, BER STREET 1891 28162

Did You Know?
NORWICH
A MISCELLANY

NORWICH, ERPINGHAM GATE 1891 28155

34

Photograph 28155 (opposite) shows the Erpingham Gate in Norwich, named after Thomas Erpingham who fought at the Battle of Agincourt in 1415. This gate was built at his expense after his death in 1428: it bears his coat of arms, and his kneeling figure appears in the niche over the arch. Erpingham is mentioned in Shakespeare's 'Henry V'.

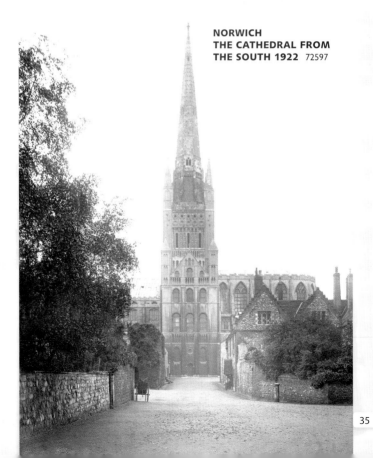

NORWICH
THE CATHEDRAL FROM
THE SOUTH 1922 72597

**THORPE ST ANDREW
THE RIVER YARE
1919** 69075

SPORTING NORWICH

Georgian Norwich was renowned for its bare-knuckle fighters. One of these was Thomas Algar, who ran the Three Crowns pub in Ber Street – known as 'the Norfolk Hero', he died in 1774 at the early age of 37. Another well-known local bare-knuckle boxer was Ned Painter who ran the Sun and Anchor in Lobster Lane in the 1820s, but perhaps the most famous fighter of all from the city was Jem Mace, the landlord of the Swan tavern in Swan Lane (where there is now a plaque to him), who was the bare-knuckle boxing champion of the world. Jem Mace became the world-champion bare-knuckle fighter for the first time in 1862 when he fought Tom King, a man almost twice his size. The fight lasted 43 rounds, and by the end Mace's right arm was damaged and he could only fight using his left arm. In 1870 Jem Mace travelled to America to fight Tom Allen for the world-champion title in Kenner, a suburb of New Orleans (prize fighting was not allowed in the city itself). The prize was 10,000 dollars and Mace won in the tenth round.

Cock fighting was also popular in the city in the Georgian period. There was a cockpit at the White Swan in the 1820s and no fewer than five pits all operating at once in the Maid's Head.

For many people, the main sporting story of Norwich is the tale of its football club. Norwich City was originally formed as an amateur club in 1902. Their ground was on Newmarket Road. In December 1904 a Football Association committee suspended three players for receiving payments and expenses. The club decided to turn professional and entered the Southern League in 1905. By 1908 City had outgrown Newmarket Road and moved to a new stadium, the Nest, in an old chalk working in Rosary Road. Behind one goal was a concrete wall, and people watched the match from the terrace above

it. In 1935 a new ground at Carrow Road was built in the two months between the end of one season and the start of the next. City's best years came in the early 1990s under the management of Mike – 'St Michael' – Walker. Norwich were contenders for the first ever Premier League title, eventually finishing third and qualifying for Europe for the first time. Their greatest triumph came when they took on the mighty Bayern Munich in Germany and beat them 2-1. In the next round Norwich met another European giant, Inter Milan. They did themselves proud, losing both matches 1-0. One of the heroes of these games was the goalkeeper Bryan Gunn. He came from Scotland but stayed on in Norwich after the end of his playing career, serving the football club and the community – he was Sheriff of Norwich for a year.

One of the finest goals in football history was scored at Carrow Road by Justin Fashanu against Liverpool in 1980. Deservedly, it was voted the BBC Match of the Day goal of the season. In the following year Justin Fashanu became the first black player to cost £1 million when he was bought from Norwich City by Brian Clough, the manager of Nottingham Forest.

NORWICH, EATON PARK YACHT POND 1932 85110

Norwich City were founder members of the Premier League in 1992-93 and played in its first three seasons before being relegated. In May 2004 the return of the club into the Premier League was celebrated by a 50,000-strong crowd who thronged the streets on a sunny evening to watch their team tour the city centre, but sadly the Canaries only stayed in the Premier League for the 2004-05 season before being relegated again. To the delight of fans, after a six-year absence the Canaries returned to the Premier League for the 2011-12 season, after finishing as runner up in the Championship in 2010-11 and winning automatic promotion.

Norwich City maintain a fierce rivalry with their East Anglian neighbours Ipswich Town. When the two clubs meet, the occasion is called the 'East Anglian Derby' but is also known as 'The Old Farm Derby', a joking reference to the name of famous 'Old Firm Derby' played between Celtic and Rangers in Scotland.

The nickname of Norwich City Football Club was originally 'The Cits' (short for 'Citizens'), but the current nickname of 'The Canaries' seems to have come into use during the 1906-07 season, probably a reference to the canary rearing that Norwich was famous for. When City played in their new strip of yellow shirts for the first time in the following season, one local newspaper marked the event with the comment 'The Cits are dead, but the Canaries are very much alive'.

The Norwich City supporters' song, 'On the ball, City', is the oldest football song anywhere in the world which is still in use today.

> *Kick it off, throw it in, have a little scrimmage,*
> *Keep it low, a splendid rush, bravo, win or die;*
> *On the ball, City, never mind the danger,*
> *Steady on, now's your chance,*
> *Hurrah! We've scored a goal, City! City! City!*

NORWICH, ELM HILL,
FIRST MAYOR OF NORWICH HOUSE (1566)
1929 81804

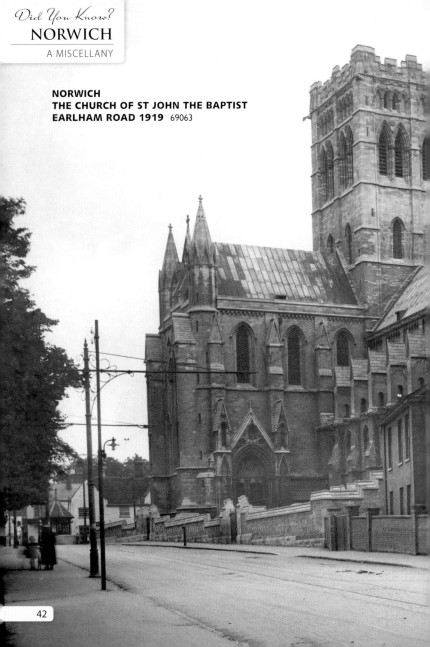

NORWICH
A MISCELLANY

Did You Know?

NORWICH

**NORWICH
THE CHURCH OF ST JOHN THE BAPTIST
EARLHAM ROAD 1919** 69063

QUIZ QUESTIONS

Answers on page 48.

1. What is the connection between Norwich and a famous fictional black horse?

2. What is the connection between Norwich and the Beatles' ground-breaking album 'Sergeant Pepper's Lonely Hearts Club Band' of 1967?

3. Photograph 81819 on the opposite page shows the memorial to local heroine Edith Cavell in Norwich, in its original (1918) position in the middle of Tombland (it has since been moved to a plot beside the cathedral precinct's Erpingham Gate). For what is Edith Cavell remembered?

4. What military device was invented at Taverham Hall during the Second World War?

5. Who designed the Norwich War Memorial, seen in photograph 81799 on page 11?

6. Who was Jenny Lind, after whom the Jenny Lind Children's Department at the Norfolk and Norwich University Hospital is named?

7. What is the origin of the unusual name of Unthank Road in Norwich?

8. A work believed to be the first book ever written in English by a woman was produced in Norwich in the 14th century. What was this, and who wrote it?

9. Where in the Norwich area can you find a statue of the Norwich Market character Billy Bluelight, and what was he famous for?

10. With which cities in the world is Norwich twinned?

NORWICH, NURSE CAVELL'S MEMORIAL
1929 81819

RECIPE

NELSON SQUARES

This recipe recalls one of Norfolk's most famous sons, Admiral Lord Nelson, who was born at Burnham Thorpe near King's Lynn in 1758. A commemorative statue of Lord Nelson stands in the cathedral close at Norwich. Replace the mixed peel with an extra 50g/2oz of dried fruit, if preferred.

    225g/8oz stale white bread, with crusts removed
    300ml/ ½ pint milk
    115g/4oz currants or raisins, or a mixture of both
    50g/2oz mixed peel, finely chopped
    50g/2oz suet
    50g/2oz demerara sugar
    1-2 level teaspoonfuls mixed spice, to taste
    1 egg for the mixture
    500g/1 lb shortcrust pastry or puff pastry
    1 beaten egg or a little extra milk for sealing and glazing the pastry

Soak the bread in the milk for half an hour, then beat out any lumps to leave a smooth mixture. Add the dried fruit, mixed peel, suet, sugar and mixed spice and mix well. Mix in the egg, and add a little extra milk if the mixture is too stiff to spread easily.

Pre-heat the oven to 180°C/350°F/Gas Mark 4. Grease a deep 22cm (9 inch) square baking tin. Roll out the pastry and cut into two sections, making one approx 28cm (11 inches) square, and the other approx 22cm (9 inches) square. Use the bigger section to line the base of the baking tin – the pastry should come up the sides of the tin. Spread the fruit mixture evenly over the pastry in the tin, leaving a slight gap around the sides. Brush the edge of the pastry with some of the beaten egg or milk, cover the mixture with the other square of pastry and pinch the edges together with the bottom layer to seal them together and enclose the mixture. Brush the surface with milk or beaten egg and prick some holes in the surface with a fork. Bake in the oven for 1½ to 2 hours, until the pastry is golden brown. Leave to cool in the tin then turn out, sprinkle with sugar and cut into squares before serving.

RECIPE

NORFOLK FAIR BUTTONS

These small, crunchy biscuits, flavoured with lemon and ginger, were traditionally sold at fairs throughout the county, including the Easter Fair held at Norwich.

> 225g/8oz plain flour
> Half a teaspoonful of ground ginger
> Half a teaspoonful of bicarbonate of soda
> 50g/2oz butter, margarine or lard, cut into small pieces
> 115g/4oz soft dark brown sugar
> 2 tablespoonfuls golden syrup
> Grated rind of 1 lemon

Pre-heat the oven to 180°C/350°F/Gas Mark 4.

Sift together the flour, ground ginger, and bicarbonate of soda into a mixing bowl. Use your fingertips to rub in the butter, margarine or lard until the mixture resembles fine breadcrumbs. Add the sugar, grated lemon rind and the golden syrup and mix it all together thoroughly to form a firm dough (the golden syrup can be warmed slightly before being added, to make it easier to mix, if preferred). Roll out the dough on a lightly floured surface, and cut into small rounds about 5cm (2 inches) in diameter. Place the rounds onto greased baking sheets, spaced well apart, and bake in the pre-heated oven for about 10-12 minutes, until they are golden brown.

Carefully lift the biscuits off the sheets using a palette knife, and leave them to cool on wire rack. They will become crispy as they cool. Store in an airtight container.

1. The connection is the classic book 'Black Beauty' written by Anna Sewell, who lived at the village of Old Catton, now a suburb of Norwich, from 1866 until her death in 1878. In 1834, when she was 14, Anna slipped and twisted her ankle: it never healed and she was ill for the rest of her life. She wrote just one book, and that not until she was 57 years old. 'Black Beauty', published in 1877, sold over a million copies in the next 15 years, and has sold at least 40 million copies since. It was written to protest against cruelty to horses, and the book did its job – animal welfare campaigners gave out free copies to stable-hands and cab-drivers. Anna knew she would not live to see the book's success, since she started writing it after her doctor had given her 18 months to live, and she died just four months after the book was published. Anna Sewell is remembered in Norwich in the name of Sewell Park (laid out from land donated by the Sewell family), Sewell Road, and the Sewell Barn Theatre in the grounds of Sewell Park College.

2. The connection is the reference to Pablo Fanque in the song 'Being for the Benefit of Mr Kite' on the album: 'The Hendersons will all be there, Late of Pablo Fanque's Fair…'. Pablo Fanque was a famous circus proprietor of the 19th century, but his real name was William Darby, born in Norwich and christened in All Saints' Church on 28 February 1796, and almost certainly the only Norwich-born person to feature in a Beatles' lyric! William Darby was the child of a mixed marriage – his father, John Darby, was a black man who worked as a butler. William became an orphan while young and was eventually apprenticed to a circus, taking the name of Pablo Fanque. He was a tightrope walker and horseman, and eventually became the first black man in Britain to become the proprietor of a circus company. John Lennon wrote the song after seeing an old poster for Pablo Fanque's circus for sale in an antique shop.

3. The First World War broke out on 4 August 1914. One person from Norwich who achieved international fame for her wartime activity was Edith Cavell, born in Swardeston in 1875. She became a nurse, working in a hospital in Brussels, but was on a visit to her mother in College Road when the war began. Despite this, Edith returned to her work in Brussels and stayed on when the Germans occupied the city. She helped many Allied soldiers escape from Belgium, and for this she was shot by the Germans on 12 October 1915. Her body was returned to England after the war, and she is buried beside the Cathedral.

4. During the Second World War Taverham Hall was taken over by the Royal Engineers, and the Bailey bridge was invented there. This device was instrumental in getting troops across the rivers of Europe after D-Day.

5. Norwich's war memorial was originally on the east face of the Guildhall, and was formally consecrated just a year before photograph 81799 (page 11) was taken. Its designer was Sir Edward Lutyens, who was also responsible for the Cenotaph in Whitehall in London. Ten years later the memorial was moved to its present setting in front of the brand-new City Hall.

6. Jenny Lind was a world-famous Swedish opera singer in the 19th century, and was popularly known as 'the Swedish Nightingale'. A major event in the local calendar is the Norfolk and Norwich Triennial Festival, which has been held every third year since 1824. Jenny Lind was paid £1,000 for her first appearance at the festival in 1847, and at a later concert, held in 1856, £2,400 was raised. Jenny Lind gave the money from both these concerts to found the children's hospital in Norwich, which was named the Lind Infirmary in her honour. The hospital was originally in Pottergate, until a new building was opened on Unthank Road in

1900. When the Lind Infirmary closed in 1975, children's services were transferred to the Norfolk and Norwich Hospital in St Stephen's Road, as the Jenny Lind Children's Department. When the new Norfolk and Norwich University Hospital was established in 2001, the Jenny Lind Children's Department moved with it.

7. The name of Unthank Road always intrigues visitors to Norwich. It is named after an early commuter to the city, William Unthank, who had a house in Eaton 200 years ago. He died in 1837 and was buried in the church of St Bartholomew in Heigham (most of which was destroyed by enemy bombing in the Second World War) where the inscription on a memorial tablet erected by his son described him as 'the zealous friend of freedom, humanity, and justice, benevolent to all, rigid in nothing but the discharge of his duty'.

8. During the medieval period there were several large monastic institutions in Norwich, including the friary of the Dominican or Black Friars, but just one house for nuns, at Carrow. One of the most important English religious mystics of the Middle Ages was Julian of Norwich, who was probably educated by the nuns of Carrow. She became an anchorite (a hermit living in a cell attached to the church, who engaged herself in contemplative prayer) at St Julian's Church on King Street. She produced a number of religious tracts, but her major work was 'Revelations of Divine Love' (or 'A Revelation of Love – in Sixteen Shewings), believed to be the first book written in English by a woman. Julian became renowned throughout England as a spiritual authority, and her saying 'All shall be well and all shall be well and all manner of thing shall be well' is still one of the most famous lines in Catholic theological writing.

9. 'Billy Bluelight' was the nickname of a well-known character from Norwich Market in the past, whose real name was William Cullum. In summer he sold flowers on the Walk for a penny a bunch. He sold hot chestnuts in autumn, cough remedies in the winter and matches, which was probably the origin of his nickname of 'Billy Bluelight'. He was also famous for racing the 'Jenny Lind', a tourist boat, along the river between Bramerton and Norwich in the 1920s and 30s. He died in 1949 and is commemorated with a statue of him racing along on the Wherryman's Way at Bramerton, as well as a plaque on a seat on the river walk, in front of the railway station.

10. Norwich is officially twinned with Novi Sad in Serbia, Rouen in France and Koblenz in Germany, and has an unofficial link with El Viejo in Nicaragua.

NORWICH, MARKET PLACE AND ST PETER MANCROFT CHURCH 1891 29133

Did You Know?
NORWICH
A MISCELLANY

**NORWICH, RAMPANT HORSE STREET
1891** 28163

COLMAN

FRANCIS FRITH

PIONEER VICTORIAN PHOTOGRAPHER

Francis Frith, founder of the world-famous photographic archive, was a complex and multi-talented man. A devout Quaker and a highly successful Victorian businessman, he was philosophical by nature and pioneering in outlook. By 1855 he had already established a wholesale grocery business in Liverpool, and sold it for the astonishing sum of £200,000, which is the equivalent today of over £15,000,000. Now in his thirties, and captivated by the new science of photography, Frith set out on a series of pioneering journeys up the Nile and to the Near East.

INTRIGUE AND EXPLORATION

He was the first photographer to venture beyond the sixth cataract of the Nile. Africa was still the mysterious 'Dark Continent', and Stanley and Livingstone's historic meeting was a decade into the future. The conditions for picture taking confound belief. He laboured for hours in his wicker dark-room in the sweltering heat of the desert, while the volatile chemicals fizzed dangerously in their trays. Back in London he exhibited his photographs and was 'rapturously cheered' by members of the Royal Society. His reputation as a photographer was made overnight.

VENTURE OF A LIFE-TIME

By the 1870s the railways had threaded their way across the country, and Bank Holidays and half-day Saturdays had been made obligatory by Act of Parliament. All of a sudden the working man and his family were able to enjoy days out, take holidays, and see a little more of the world.

With typical business acumen, Francis Frith foresaw that these new tourists would enjoy having souvenirs to commemorate their days out. For the next thirty years he travelled the country by train and by pony and trap, producing fine photographs of seaside resorts and beauty spots that were keenly bought by millions of Victorians. These prints were painstakingly pasted into family albums and pored over during the dark nights of winter, rekindling precious memories of summer excursions. Frith's studio was soon supplying retail shops all over the country, and by 1890 F Frith & Co had become the greatest specialist photographic publishing company in the world, with over 2,000 sales outlets, and pioneered the picture postcard.

FRANCIS FRITH'S LEGACY

Francis Frith had died in 1898 at his villa in Cannes, his great project still growing. By 1970 the archive he created contained over a third of a million pictures showing 7,000 British towns and villages.

Frith's legacy to us today is of immense significance and value, for the magnificent archive of evocative photographs he created provides a unique record of change in the cities, towns and villages throughout Britain over a century and more. Frith and his fellow studio photographers revisited locations many times down the years to update their views, compiling for us an enthralling and colourful pageant of British life and character.

We are fortunate that Frith was dedicated to recording the minutiae of everyday life. For it is this sheer wealth of visual data, the painstaking chronicle of changes in dress, transport, street layouts, buildings, housing and landscape that captivates us so much today, offering us a powerful link with the past and with the lives of our ancestors.

Computers have now made it possible for Frith's many thousands of images to be accessed almost instantly. The archive offers every one of us an opportunity to examine the places where we and our families have lived and worked down the years. Its images, depicting our shared past, are now bringing pleasure and enlightenment to millions around the world a century and more after his death.

For further information visit: www.francisfrith.com

INTERIOR DECORATION

Frith's photographs can be seen framed and as giant wall murals in thousands of pubs, restaurants, hotels, banks, retail stores and other public buildings throughout Britain. These provide interesting and attractive décor, generating strong local interest and acting as a powerful reminder of gentler days in our increasingly busy and frenetic world.

FRITH PRODUCTS

All Frith photographs are available as prints and posters in a variety of different sizes and styles. In the UK we also offer a range of other gift and stationery products illustrated with Frith photographs, although many of these are not available for delivery outside the UK – see our web site for more information on the products available for delivery in your country.

THE INTERNET

Over 100,000 photographs of Britain can be viewed and purchased on the Frith web site. The web site also includes memories and reminiscences contributed by our customers, who have personal knowledge of localities and of the people and properties depicted in Frith photographs. If you wish to learn more about a specific town or village you may find these reminiscences fascinating to browse. Why not add your own comments if you think they would be of interest to others? See **www.francisfrith.com**

PLEASE HELP US BRING FRITH'S PHOTOGRAPHS TO LIFE

Our authors do their best to recount the history of the places they write about. They give insights into how particular towns and villages developed, they describe the architecture of streets and buildings, and they discuss the lives of famous people who lived there. But however knowledgeable our authors are, the story they tell is necessarily incomplete.

Frith's photographs are so much more than plain historical documents. They are living proofs of the flow of human life down the generations. They show real people at real moments in history; and each of those people is the son or daughter of someone, the brother or sister, aunt or uncle, grandfather or grandmother of someone else. All of them lived, worked and played in the streets depicted in Frith's photographs.

We would be grateful if you would give us your insights into the places shown in our photographs: the streets and buildings, the shops, businesses and industries. Post your memories of life in those streets on the Frith website: what it was like growing up there, who ran the local shop and what shopping was like years ago; if your workplace is shown tell us about your working day and what the building is used for now. Read other visitors' memories and reconnect with your shared local history and heritage. With your help more and more Frith photographs can be brought to life, and vital memories preserved for posterity, and for the benefit of historians in the future.

Wherever possible, we will try to include some of your comments in future editions of our books. Moreover, if you spot errors in dates, titles or other facts, please let us know, because our archive records are not always completely accurate—they rely on 140 years of human endeavour and hand-compiled records. You can email us using the contact form on the website.

Thank you!

For further information, trade, or author enquiries
please contact us at the address below:

**The Francis Frith Collection, Oakley Business Park,
Wylye Road, Dinton, Wiltshire SP3 5EU.**
Tel: +44 (0)1722 716 376 Fax: +44 (0)1722 716 881
e-mail: sales@francisfrith.co.uk **www.francisfrith.com**